Crafting a Social Media Strategy for Public Relations

Table of Contents

Social media is not just an activity; it is an investment of valuable time and resources. Surround yourself with people who not just support you and stay with you, but inform your thinking about ways to WOW your online presence

— Sean Gardner

Chapter 1. Introduction

In the era of digital communications, mastering an effective social media strategy has become a critical gear in the public relations machinery. Our Special Report, 'Crafting a Social Media Strategy for Public Relations,' provides an extensive, yet easy-to-understand roadmap for navigating this crucial aspect. This report does not demand any high-grade technical knowledge and is adorned with a lively and motivating narrative, promising to engage you from start to finish. It is the robust guide you need to understand the dynamics, devise sharp strategies, and ultimately drive flourishing interactions on various social platforms. Grab your copy today and unlock the endless potential of social media for your public relations endeavors. Happy strategizing!

Chapter 2. Understanding the Landscape of Social Media

In the dawn of the information age, we first embark on our journey by understanding the landscape of social media. Comparative to explorers charting out new terrains, our aim here is to grasp the broad outlines in one of the most significant innovations of our time, social media.

2.1. Dissecting the Social Media

When it comes to social media, we can't limit our understanding to a handful of platforms. From the blogging empire of WordPress, the evanescent sharing realm of Snapchat, to the scrolling plethora of Pinterest boards, a myriad of social networks sprawl across our digital tales. Each network is unique, serving a distinct purpose, and attracting a separate demographic. Yet, they all share a common core; they offer a platform for user-generated content, open doors to real-time interaction, and reinforce digital footprints primarily of individuals but also of businesses and organizations.

Facebook, for instance, began as a communication tool for college students but rapidly evolved into a global social network engulfing individuals of all ages, businesses, and organizations worldwide. Twitter, with its inherent brevity, champions real-time information, thus becoming a hub for news, updates, and quick-fire dialogues. Instagram captures life through images and videos, making it a hotspot for personal storytelling, lifestyle sharing, and visual marketing. LinkedIn serves as our online professional network, a virtual resume, and a hub for thought leadership.

All these platforms provide cooperative connectivity; they thrive on user engagement, comments, tags, shares, reactions, all of which collectively form our social media landscape. It's a gradient, an ecosystem, an intensely human digital invention that captures and reflects our behavioral nuances.

2.2. The Mechanism of Social Media

The concept of social media is nestled within Web 2.0, the phase of internet evolution characterized by participatory information sharing, interoperability, and user-centered design. In this context, social media operates, by and large, on three fundamental principles: conversation, community, and content.

Conversation pertains to the communication aspect of social media. It's the lifeline that keeps the social aspect of social media alive. It's the likes, comments, shares, retweets, and mentions that gives a post vitality and augments its reach.

Community refers to the clustering of individuals with shared interests. It's the Facebook and LinkedIn groups, Twitter chats, Pinterest boards, and Instagram hashtags bringing together a community of people rallied behind a common cause, belief, or preference.

Content is the heart of any social media platform. Text, photos, videos, and links, it's through these modes of content that conversation and community are fueled. Content strategy, therefore, becomes paramount in harnessing the potential of social media.

2.3. From Social-First to Mobile-First

While social media was a radical shift in itself, the pivot of the digital world towards mobile-first has had profound impacts on the social media landscape. Today, most social media usage is through smartphones. The ease of access, real-time updates, and the on-the-go nature of social media interaction sync perfectly with our mobile culture. Apps have revolutionized the distribution and consumption layers of social media. This shift necessitates mobile-optimized content, a key marker in understanding current social media dynamics.

2.4. Privacy in the Social Media Age

In the vast spread of social media platforms emerges a critical issue, privacy. The complexity and magnitude of data that social media platforms collect and process have raised significant concerns about personal privacy and data protection. This understanding is crucial when navigating the social media landscape, especially for businesses and organizations. It's not merely about using the platform; it's also about understanding the framework you operate within, respecting privacy laws, and safeguarding your digital identity.

Armed with this understanding of its landscape, we can now delve deeper into harnessing social media as a powerful tool for public relations, weaving meaningful interactions with users and fostering a brand narrative that resonates with your audience. Unfurl the sails; we are about to set course in the world of social media strategy.

Chapter 3. The Importance of Public Relations in the Social Media Age

In this new era marked by the pervasive influence of technology and the internet, it's undeniable that public relations (PR) has evolved significantly, adapting itself to the massive shift led by social media. Traditional PR practices have been transformed, making room for a broader conversation, timely responsiveness, and a dynamic interaction between brands and their audiences. This chapter would emphasize the criticality of PR in the age of social media, elucidating the key shifts in the landscape and elucidating how to leverage them effectively.

3.1. The Evolution of PR in the Digital Age

Understanding the emergence and impact of PR in the social media age necessitates a brief examination of its evolution. Traditional PR practices focused on one-directional communication, primarily utilizing press releases, newsletters, and media briefing to deliver messages to the public. However, the digital revolution signaled by Web 2.0, led to democratization of information and birth of social media platforms, exponentially increasing the speed, scale, and scope of information dissemination. This resulted in PR transitioning from controlling the message to facilitating dialogues, requiring novel strategies to engage audiences in real-time conversations, address concerns, and manage brand reputation.

3.2. Relevance of PR for Branding in the Social Media Age

The advent of social media not only altered the PR landscape, it also critically changed branding strategies. With social media platforms empowering consumers to have a voice, brands often find their reputation shaped significantly by customer experiences shared online. Given this development, PR is no longer only about managing press releases but further includes listening to online discourse, timely responding to feedback, and appropriately influencing public opinion to maintain a positive brand image. When well-executed, PR in the social media age can result in strengthening brand identity, improving audience engagement, and ultimately elevating overall brand equity.

3.3. The PR - Social Media Synergy

Neglecting social media is no longer viable for PR professionals. There is an intrinsic, powerful tie between PR and social media, each enhancing the efficacy of the other. Social media provides PR with a platform to directly engage with audiences, offering a quicker response time and personalized interaction. In contrast, PR adds immense value to social media campaigns by integrating strategic narratives, underlining key messaging, and further driving constructive dialogue. This harmony between social media and PR is therefore the cornerstone of effective public relations in the digital age.

3.4. Navigating the Challenges

Despite numerous potential benefits, employing social media in PR efforts isn't without complications. The same transparency that allows brands to construct an authentic relationship with their audience also makes them vulnerable to online crises that can quickly escalate. There's also the challenge of information overload, where a brand's message can get lost amidst the constant influx of content. PR professionals must strategically navigate through these challenges, ensuring the right message reaches the right audience at the right time, thereby deftly managing their brand's reputation.

In summary, PR in the social media age is a dynamic, interactive process, vastly different from the traditional PR practice of one-way communication. By successfully leveraging this transition, PR professionals can harness the power of social media to strengthen their brand reputation, engage with their audience on a more personal level, and create a meaningful dialogue that fosters trust and strengthens brand relationships.

3.5. Looking Ahead

The digital landscape and with it, the realm of PR and social media, is ever-evolving. Embracing this inevitability, PR professionals must consistently stay updated with the latest trends, adapt their strategies accordingly, and strive for innovation in their communication efforts. It's crucial to remember that though the tools might change, the core principle of PR remains the same – building and maintaining fruitful relationships with one's publics. Mastering the art of effectively adapting PR strategies to different platforms and contexts is therefore the key to thriving in the social media age. The chapters ahead will delve deeper into these aspects, guiding readers on creating compelling social media content, leveraging different platforms and managing online crises – all essential components of a robust, modern PR strategy.

Chapter 4. Developing a Strategic Vision for Social Media Engagement

Understanding the essence of effective social media engagement involves more than simply being active on various platforms. It involves developing a strategic vision that drives your public relations program well into the digital age and beyond. This vision, much like a compass, guides your interactions, the content you share, and even how you respond to the feedback you receive. It's a critical component of your overall social media strategy, influencing every action and decision you make.

4.1. The Importance of a Strategic Vision

A strategic vision for social media engagement is essentially your guiding light. The digital landscape is constantly shifting, and new trends and platforms emerge frequently. As such, having a strategic vision keeps your efforts focused and aligned. It outlines what you want to achieve, who you'd like to reach, how you intend to do this, and how you'll measure the success of your efforts.

Without it, you may find that your efforts are scattered and ineffective, leading to a waste of valuable resources like time and money. It's not unlike a ship sailing without a clear direction: sure, it might eventually get somewhere, but it will likely have wasted a lot of fuel and time along the way.

4.2. Crafting Your Strategic Vision

The process of crafting a strategic vision for your social media engagement involves several steps.

Step 1: Identify your Goals — This is the "what" of your strategy. What do you want to achieve through social media engagement? Generate leads? Enhance brand recognition? Boost sales? Foster relationships? The clearer your goals, the easier it will be to craft a vision that aligns with them.

Step 2: Know your Audience — Understanding who you're trying to reach forms the "who" of your vision. Are they millennials or Gen Z? Are they tech-savvy or prefer traditional media? Knowing your audience will affect your tone, content, platform choice, etc.

Step 3: Choose your Platforms — Different platforms attract different users and are better suited for different types of content. This is your "where." For example, Instagram and Pinterest are great for visual content, while LinkedIn is more suitable for professional and business-related content.

Step 4: Content Strategy — This covers the "what" you'll be sharing to engage with your audience. Should your content be educational, entertaining, inspiring, or a mix of these? The answer depends on your goals and your audience.

Step 5: Analysis and Feedback — This is how you'll measure the success of your efforts and get feedback. It involves setting up Key Performance Indicators (KPIs) to monitor, and tools to garner feedback from your audience.

4.3. Syncing Your Vision with Your Overall Business Strategy

It's critical that your strategic vision for social media engagement aligns with your overall business strategy. All elements of your organization — from product development to marketing to customer service — should work in tandem toward common goals. If your social media engagement strategy isn't synced with your overall business objectives, you risk sending disjointed messages to your audience and wasting resources on ineffective initiatives.

4.4. Constantly Refining Your Strategic Vision

Remember, your strategic vision isn't set in stone. Just as the digital landscape evolves, so should your vision. Regularly review and refine your strategic vision to ensure that it remains aligned with your goals, reflects changes in your audience's behaviors and preferences, and allows you to leverage the potential of new platforms and trends.

In conclusion, developing a robust strategic vision for social media engagement is a process that requires clear goal-setting, an in-depth understanding of your audience, strategic platform and content choices, thorough analysis and feedback mechanisms, alignment with overall business strategy, and a commitment to continuous refinement. With this framework, your social media activities will not simply be reactionary responses to the landscape's shifts but will be deliberate, strategic actions driving your public relations endeavors forward. Having a strategic vision helps ensure every step you take on the social platforms brings you closer to your outlined goals, contributing to more purposeful, efficient, and effective engagement.

Chapter 5. Understanding Your Audience: Market Research in the Digital Age

No discipline or industry has remained untouched by the transformative wave of digitalization, and market research is no exception. In today's digital age, where communication happens at the speed of light, possessing the ability to identify, comprehend, and connect with your audience in a genuine and meaningful manner is a business imperative. This chapter will serve as your guide, conceptualizing the intersection of market research and digital progress, thereby facilitating the development of potent strategies to resonate with your audience on social media platforms.

5.1. The Essence of Knowing Your Audience

Understanding the construct of your audience is the cornerstone of any successful social media strategy. However, this task is more multifaceted than you might think. It's not enough to merely know demographic facts about your audience, such as their gender, age, profession, or geographical location. While these details undoubtedly contribute to fashioning your audience persona, they do not apprehend the entirety of your audience's identity. You must delve deeper and unearth their interests, preferences, beliefs, seeking to grasp what they value, what problems they incur, the products or services they desire, and what motivates them to engage online.

5.2. Leveraging Technology for Audience Insights

In the technology-driven era, we are surrounded by virtual mountains of data, developed every second, from every corner of the world. This data includes a wealth of knowledge about your audience—what they click, which sites they visit, how much time they spend online, and many other aspects of their digital lives. Various tools and software have emerged, specializing in data mining, data analysis, and reporting that can help you to collect, analyze, and interpret this sea of information.

Google Analytics, Facebook Insights, Twitter Analytics, and many others offer free or affordable data analysis tools that can provide you comprehensive insight into your audience's behavior and preferences. Alongside, standalone tools such as Sprout Social, Hootsuite, and Buzzsumo can help you delve deeper into the social data.

5.3. Original Research

In addition to leveraging the existent data, you can conduct original research to gather primary data about your audience. Methods such as online surveys, polls on social media platforms, interviews, or focus group discussions can provide an unfiltered understanding of your audience.

By gaining first-hand insights, you can make informed decisions about your social media strategy, thereby increasing the chances of resonating with your audience.

5.4. The Role of Analytics in Profiling Audience

Analytics takes these efforts a notch higher. Businesses can employ analytics to not only describe their current audience but also predict future trends. Analytics teams can use machine learning and artificial intelligence to spot patterns in large datasets, generating insights that would have otherwise gone unnoticed.

Engaging with Alexa rankings or Similarweb can indicate where your audience comes from, the kind of content they consume frequently, and for how long they engage—offering essential metrics for your social media strategy.

5.5. Developing Audience Personas

Once you collect and analyze the data, your next step is to create audience personas—a semi-fictional characterization of your ideal customer based on the research.

This helps you visualize your audience, allowing you to create and tailor content that would resonate with them personally, thereby fostering increased engagement.

5.6. Incorporating Your Findings into content strategy

The next and most important step is to align the insights from your audience research into your content strategy. This involves creating posts that appeal to your followers based on their interests, needs, and preferences.

By engaging in scheduled posts, you ensure consistent communication with your audience, keeping them informed, entertained, and enthralled. The eventual goal is not only for your content to resonate, but also to inspire your audience to share your posts, extending your reach, traffic, and engagement.

5.7. Conclusion

In conclusion, understanding your audience is not as straightforward in the digital age. However, by adeptly leveraging the available rich data streams, advanced technologies for audience insights, original research initiatives, robust analytics, audience personas, and an audience-focused content strategy, you can indeed comprehend your audience at an unparalleled level. This understanding, undoubtedly, paves the way for a successful social media strategy, which can drive flourishing interactions and reap significant business benefits in the long run.

Chapter 6. Creating Compelling Content: The Lifeblood of Social Media Strategy

All good narratives begin with a compelling story, and in the age of digital media, your story needs to be not just heard, but experienced. This unravelled narrative will guide you in crafting compelling content—the veritable lifeblood of any effective social media strategy.

6.1. Crafting Your Brand's Story

Every brand has its unique story—a story that separates it from the crowd. Understanding and communicating your brand's narrative is the initial step in crafting compelling content. Your brand's narrative needs to articulate who you are, what you represent, and why your brand matters. It should connect with your audience on a shared set of values and experiences. Take Patagonia, for example. Its brand story isn't about clothing; it's about a love for the outdoors and a commitment to environmental conservation. All its content communicates this narrative, effectively connecting with and engaging its specific target group.

6.2. Understanding What Resonates with Your Audience

Knowing your audience is an indispensable element of delivering engaging content. You need a clear and detailed understanding of your audience's demographics, psychographics, and behavioral characteristics. Incorporate tools like Facebook Insights, Google Analytics, or customer analytics dashboards to aid in understanding your audience better. These platforms provide insights into trending topics, user behavior, and content preferences among your audience, allowing you to further refine your messaging and content creation strategy for a more effective engagement.

6.3. Emphasizing Visual Appeal

In a world where attention spans are waning, and information overload is the norm, visual content stands out. Human brains process visual data up to 60,000 times faster than text-based information. Research shows posts with visuals receive 94% more page visits and engagements than those without. With this in mind, your content strategy should involve the use of images, infographics, videos, animations, and other graphic elements to capture your audience's attention and convey your brand's story effectively.

6.4. Harnessing the Power of User-Generated Content (UGC)

Today's consumers trust peer reviews and user-generated content more than traditional advertising. UGC encourages users to share their experiences or engage with your brand, creating a sense of community, authenticity, and trust. Encouraging your followers to generate content allows you to establish strong audience relationships, gain user trust, and benefit from increased engagement rates. Remember to always give credit to the original content creator; this encourages others to contribute and protects your brand against any copyright infringements.

6.5. Creating an Editorial Calendar

A planned approach to social media posts ensures consistency, which is key in maintaining audience engagement. Your content calendar should align with your branding strategy, key promotional events, and consumer behavior patterns. This calendar can include content types, post times, intended platforms, associated metrics, and responsible team members. Moreover, it has the additional advantage of allowing you to prepare and polish your content in advance, thereby ensuring utmost quality.

6.6. Engaging through Social Listening

Your content strategy must not be solely focused on speaking; listening is equally essential. Social listening involves tracking conversations around specific phrases, words, or brands, and leveraging these insights to create content your audience will resonate with. Tools like Mention, Hootsuite, or Brandwatch can aid you in tracking relevant data on audience preferences, competitor strategies, trending topics, and key influencers in your domain.

6.7. Experimenting and Evolving

Creating compelling content is an art, but it's also a science. This involves testing, learning, and refining your approach. A/B testing is a popular method to understand what resonates best with your audience. Over time, you will gain insights to tweak and improve your content strategy, adapting to emerging trends and changing platform algorithms.

In conclusion, creating compelling content is not just about crafting a catchy post. It is about understanding your audience, your brand, and the context in which the conversation is happening. It's about creativity, strategy, and data-driven decisions. It's an iterative process of learning, experimenting, and evolving. Craft your content mindfully, and watch as it becomes the beating heart of a thriving social media strategy.

Chapter 7. Leveraging Different Social Media Platforms: Strengths and Challenges

In the throes of your expedition through the land of social media strategy, you now embark on a pivotal stage - the comprehension and application of the distinct strengths and challenges across various social media platforms. To tread this landscape with confidence, one must recognize the unique attributes, audiences, and applications inherent to each platform, and align them with the communicated message of your brand, organization, or client.

7.1. The Pioneering Force: Facebook

Dominating the realm of social media since its inception in 2004, Facebook has burgeoned into a universal platform that bridges demographic territories. The platform offers a broad collection of tools for public relations, including brand pages, event creation, content sharing, engaging advertisements, and intricate analytics.

Although catering to a diverse audience, Facebook's conventional users lie within the age range of 25 to 34. The platform favors rich, engaging content, typically in the form of videos, live streams, and high-quality images accompanied by compelling narratives. Understanding that organic reach is limited due to extensive algorithms, Facebook strategy often involves a sensible blend of organic content and targeted advertisements.

Despite its breadth of features and audience reach, Facebook embodies challenges in its notoriously intricate algorithms that prioritize content from friends and family. Organizations may struggle to achieve broad reach without significant ad spend. Additionally, the platform's reputation for privacy issues can erode trust among some demographics.

7.2. The Power of Brevity: Twitter

Twitter comes with its own set of tools that lend well to amplifying your brand's voice. Broadcasting disaster management messages, real-time alerts, public announcements, or live updates becomes succinct and instant on this platform. Key demographics on Twitter are characterized by a younger audience, specifically ages 18 to 29, with a keen interest in topical discussions and trending news.

Craft a Twitter strategy by focusing on timely content, engaging in relevant conversations, incorporating popular hashtags, and developing a consistent posting schedule. The platform welcomes concise messaging accompanied by bold visuals.

However, the challenges are few but significant. The platform's rapid pace can cause content to be buried swiftly in the feed, compelling a need for constant activity, and comprehensive issues can be difficult to articulate within the constrained character limit.

7.3. Professional Playground: LinkedIn

LinkedIn emerges as an unmatched platform for B2B communication, corporate public relations, professional networking, employment branding, and industry thought leadership. The platform caters primarily to a professional audience, aged between 30 to 49 years.

An efficient LinkedIn strategy involves creating company pages, posting curated content demonstrating industry expertise, participating in relevant groups, and engaging in thoughtful conversations. Rich media like infographics or short videos assist in making content more consumable.

On the flip side, however, LinkedIn requires a meticulous engagement strategy as untargeted or excessive posting may lead to audience attrition. Further, compared to other platforms, LinkedIn's ad solutions are costlier, making it a less accessible option for smaller businesses or startups.

7.4. Aesthetic Appeal: Instagram

With its focus on visual storytelling, Instagram offers a vibrant platform for brands to showcase their personality and aesthetics. It typically attracts a younger generation, predominantly between the ages of 18 to 34, who are responsive to creative and authentic content.

An effective Instagram strategy hinges on high-quality visuals, compelling captions, regular utilization of stories, engagement with followers, and blending in sponsored content subtly. In recent years, Instagram has added features such as IGTV and Reels, allowing for longer video content that can further engage audiences.

Nevertheless, the platform's focus on aesthetically pleasing content necessitates considerable investment in resources and creativity. The reliance on this visual element may prove challenging for brands whose messaging is not naturally "image-friendly."

7.5. Rapid Connections: TikTok

TikTok, the latest addition to the social media clan, characterizes itself with user-generated short videos that appeal to a primarily young demographic - mostly under 24 years of age. It's a platform that revels in authenticity, creativity, and lighthearted content.

To effectively leverage TikTok, brands must grasp the platform's culture, trends, and challenges in content creation. It's about having a sense of humor, integrating popular music, sparking challenges, or even partnering with creators for greater reach.

However, TikTok's main challenges lie in its recent emergence, the necessity of video content, the rapid pace of trends, and its relatively young audience which may not align with all brands' target demographics.

Now that we've mapped the landscape of the major platforms, it's up to you to navigate this varied terrain with the compass of your unique brand message. Understanding each platform's strengths and challenges enables a comprehensive, effective, and dynamic social media strategy that can adapt to shifting landscapes and continually engage audiences. Remember, each platform offers a unique way to tell your story. Your aim is to tell it in a way that resonates most profoundly with your desired audiences, while making the most of the tools each platform provides.

Chapter 8. Risk Management and Crisis Communication on Social Media

Within the realm of social media communications, an indispensable facet is aptly managing risks and efficiently handling crises. It demands a careful assessment of potential hazards, preparation for contingencies, swift yet thoughtful response practices, and a comprehensive review system.

8.1. Recognizing the Risks

The first stride in managing risks is to discern and acknowledge the potential perils that may encroach upon your organization's social media presence. These threats can range from seemingly harmless customer grievances that might snowball into a public relations nightmare to serious data breaches that leak sensitive information.

The significance of minor discontentment amongst consumers should not be undermined. With the connectivity enhanced by social media, a single disgruntled customer can trigger a damaging ripple effect with the click of a mouse. And, with data becoming the new oil, technological loopholes that allow unauthorized access to confidential data can prove catastrophic. Furthermore, the risk of erroneous communication, either from inside the organization or due to misinterpretations by the audience, is ever-present.

8.2. Crafting a Crisis Communication Plan

Preparation is synonymous with prudence. Your crisis

communication plan should function as a roadmap that guides the organizational response during a crisis. This guidance should be explicit about the steps to undertake if things go awry.

Firstly, designate a crisis management team with clear demarcations of roles and responsibilities. This team should be empowered to make crucial decisions in the heat of the moment. Secondly, devise a notification system to ensure that, in crisis times, all pertinent stakeholders are informed and updated quickly. Thirdly, have a list of potential crises that may impact your organization and a corresponding plan of action for each scenario.

Moreover, transparency and honesty should lay the foundation of your crisis communication strategy. Admissions of failings may seem counterintuitive but, in the long run, they can contribute to enhancing your brand's credibility.

8.3. Reacting to Crisis Situations

When a crisis strikes, quick yet thoughtful action is what sets leading brands apart. Regardless of the predicament you are in, never allow your social media to be a silent observer.

Initially, acknowledge the crisis, even if you do not have all the answers. An honest affirmation is always better than elusiveness. Then, outline your proposed solution and detail the corrective steps you are undertaking. Remember to also manage your staff's online behavior, as everything they say can have an impact on the perception of your organization.

8.4. Post-Crisis Review

After the dust settles, conduct a thorough evaluation to understand the effectiveness of your crisis management strategy. This exercise also aids in refining your future responses and takes you one step closer to mastering your crisis communication.

Analyze how swiftly the crisis was addressed and what could have been done better. Tweaking your strategy based on these revelations will equip you even better for any crisis that you may face in the future.

8.5. Embracing Social Media for Crisis Management

Social media, despite presenting risks, can also serve as an ally during a crisis. It can provide a platform to express empathy, a tool to update consumers about corrective actions, a resource to restore consumer trust, and a channel to reach out to stakeholders swiftly and directly.

In essence, mastering risk management and crisis communication on social media is a continuous process imbued with learnings from past experiences. It involves recognizing potential hazards, crafting a proactive crisis communication plan, reacting aptly when crises occur, conducting a post-crisis review, and leveraging the utility of social media platforms themselves. It is through this meticulous process that you can turn social media risks into opportunities for trust building and, ultimately, public relations triumph.

Chapter 9. Implementing Social Media Strategy: Tools and Tactics

In the labyrinth of the social media world, establishing a strategy is equivalent to devising a map. The development of methodologies, set priorities, and defined objectives, however, is just the beginning. Now, as we herald a shift from planning to execution, we journey into the realm of specific tools and tactical approaches that can enable effective implementation of the social media strategy.

9.1. Understanding the Utilitarian Features of Social Media Tools

The modern digital era presents an elaborate toolkit teeming with diverse functionalities, designed to cater to different facets of social media strategy implementation. Some tools possess the prowess to amplify your message, engage with your audience, monitor the metrics, or automate tasks - but understanding which of these elements are particularly pertinent to your requirements forms the first step of this implementation journey.

To aid decision-making, we must delve into a broad categorisation of these tools:

- **Content Creation tools**: Tools such as Canva, Adobe Spark, and Buffer's Pablo can facilitate creating visually striking and captivating content.

- **Content Management and Scheduling tools**: These tools, including Hootsuite, Sprout Social, and Buffer, help schedule posts across multiple platforms and manage content efficiently.

- **Social Listening and Monitoring tools**: Tools like Brandwatch, Awario, and Mention can track online conversations about your brand, helping you respond promptly.

- **Analytics tools**: Tools such as Google Analytics, FollowerWonk, and Keyhole provide valuable insights about your audience and effectiveness of your promotional efforts.

Exploring these tools, understanding their functionalities, and aligning them with your specific needs can set a solid groundwork for a successful social media strategy.

9.2. Tactical Play: Crafting the Right Approach

Tool selection might form the base of the operation, but the blueprint of a successful strategy includes adept tactical maneuvering. Being tactical about the implementation of your strategy describes how to best use these tools to meet the set objectives.

The framework for this involves:

1. **Define Clear Goals**: What needs to be achieved - engagement, brand awareness, lead conversion, website traffic, or community building? Clear goals lead to focused strategies.

2. **Selection of refined tool set**: After understanding the universe of tools, invest time in precisely pinpointing the ones that comprehensively satisfy the requirements of your set goals.

3. **Developing a Content Calendar**: A well-planned content calendar can help maintain consistency, avoid redundancy, and ensure balanced content distribution. This can be achieved using scheduling tools like Buffer or Hootsuite.

4. **Measurement and Adjustment**: Establish a system to continually measure the success and impact of your efforts,

adjusting your tactics as necessary.

With a well-defined tactical methodology in place, you can navigate the social media waters effectively, driven by a clear vision, and directed towards well-defined checkpoints.

9.3. Embracing Automation: A Game-changer

A critical dimension of implementing a social media strategy is the judicious integration of automation. While maintaining personal touch and authenticity is essential, automation can streamline routines, increase efficiency and maintain a constant presence. Planning content in advance or scheduling posts using Sprout Social or Buffer, utilizing chatbots for customer conversations, automating responses to common queries can provide a significant boost to your strategy.

However, the balance needs to be struck. Over-automation might reduce the personal touch that makes social media engaging. Hence, moderation is key.

9.4. Crisis Management: Breaking Barriers

Every brand, regardless of its popularity, has potentially faced a PR crisis online. Therefore, devising a clear crisis management plan harnessing the power of social tools should form a pivotal part of the strategy.

This involves:

1. **Monitoring**: Utilize tools like Brandwatch or Mention to keep track of online conversations and sentiment about your brand.

2. **Swift and Clear Communication**: Address the crisis swiftly without inflaming the situation and notify your customers about any rectification efforts through your social channels.

3. **Analyzing Post-Crisis**: Reflect on the event, what went wrong, what was handled well, and how to prevent reoccurrences.

Implementing a social media strategy is not just about launching campaigns and measuring success. It's about knowing how to react when the going gets tough and transforming a potential crisis into an advantage.

9.5. Decoding Analytics: Learning from your Efforts

The ultimate determinant of the effectiveness of your strategy is in the data. Using analytical tools and understanding the key performance indicators can provide not just evidence of success, but also valuable insights to modify, improve, and craft more engaging campaigns in the future. Tools like Google Analytics, FollowerWonk, or Keyhole are excellent in providing this overview.

By converting these numbers into meaningful analyses, you can gauge user engagement levels, demographic breakdowns, popular content, and more. This can be a gold mine of information to tweak your strategies, amplify your reach, and attain your stated goals.

As we conclude this elaborate dive into implementing a social media strategy, remember that understanding tools and crafting tactics is an iterative process. Through constant learning, analysis and adaptation, you can truly master this digital realm and unlock the infinite potential of social media for public relations.

Chapter 10. Measuring Success: Social Media Analytics and Key Performance Indicators

The exploration of success metrics in social media strategy is not only a process of number crunching but, more importantly, serves as a compass guiding strategists towards their communication objectives. Success is measured by the extent to which efforts align with the desired outcomes. In this chapter, we prod deeper into the world of social media analytics and key performance indicators (KPIs) to provide an enriching understanding of how the fruits of a social media strategy can be weighed, evaluated, and refined.

10.1. Understanding Social Media Analytics

At the heart of measuring success in social media strategy lies the tool of analytics - a systematic computational analysis of data. Social media analytics involves the gathering, monitoring, and analysis of interaction and engagement data from various social media platforms. This data provides critical insights into how your content is resonating with your audience and impacting your business, political, or social objectives. Platforms can range from Facebook, Twitter, Instagram and LinkedIn, to YouTube, Pinterest, Reddit, and beyond.

Different platforms offer different native analytics tools (like Facebook Insights, Twitter Analytics), but there are also third-party tools available that can provide a more in-depth and cross-platform analysis - tools such as Hootsuite, Buffer, or Socialbakers.

Understanding social media analytics is like interpreting a narrative about your audience's behavior and interaction with your brand online, allowing you to track which strategies are working, which ones need re-calibration, and illuminating new opportunities.

10.2. Defining Key Performance Indicators (KPIs)

As we delve further, understanding KPIs is essential in our journey. Key Performance Indicators are quantifiable metrics that correspond to your strategic objectives. They are the benchmarks for success that tick the checkboxes of your strategic vision and validate efforts made. Essentially, KPIs are reflections of your goals in number form.

Selecting the right KPIs is crucial as improper selection can lead to inaccurate conclusions. For instance, if your objective is to improve brand awareness and reach, metrics such as 'Likes' or 'Followers' could be relevant KPIs. However, if customer engagement and interaction are your primary goals, KPIs such as 'Comments', 'Shares', and 'Average Duration of Engagement', may provide more accurate insights.

10.3. Types of Social Media Metrics

To provide a well-rounded view of your social media influence, several types of metrics are commonly considered.

1. **Vanity Metrics**: They include Likes, Follows, Comments, and Shares. They are 'feel-good' numbers that give a basic level of engagement but do not necessarily translate into business success.

2. **Engagement Metrics**: These deal with how your audience is interacting with your content — Comments, Likes, Shares, Clicks, and Average Duration of Engagement.

3. **Reach and Impressions**: Reach refers to the number of unique users exposed to your content while Impressions mean the total number of views your content receives.

4. **Referral Traffic**: This measures how much of your website traffic comes from social media platforms.

5. **Lead Generation and Conversion Rates**: These metrics measure the effectiveness of social media initiatives in driving sales and conversions.

6. **Follower Growth Rate**: It measures how fast you are gaining followers over a specific period.

10.4. Implementing and Analyzing KPIs

After defining KPIs, they must be continuously tracked, measured, and analyzed. Social media KPIs are often represented in formats such as charts, graphs, and tables for easy comprehension and comparative analysis. You can also apply data analytics techniques to derive patterns and trends in your metrics over time.

With each analysis, it's essential to reflect on your findings. If a particular KPI isn't reflecting expected results, you might have to tweak or overhaul your strategy. A lack of growth in 'Followers', for instance, might denote a need for more compelling content to attract potential followers. Alternatively, low 'Shares' might require a re-evaluation of your content's shareability and value proposition.

10.5. The Future of Measuring Success: Advanced Analytics

As social media trends shift and evolve, so must the way we measure success. Advanced analytics, predictive analytics, and AI play a larger role in understanding audience patterns and predicting future trends. Automation tools are increasingly taking over data collection and analysis, leaving strategists with more time to interpret data and finesse their strategies.

In conclusion, measuring success in social media strategy isn't just about tallying likes and shares - it's a multifaceted process that requires an understanding of social media analytics, defining relevant KPIs, and continuous tracking and improvement. From deciphering the language of metrics to predictive analysis, this process holds the key to achieving your public relations objectives across the dynamic landscape of social media platforms.

Chapter 11. Future Trends: Adapting to Changing Social Media Landscapes

As we navigate the vast plain of social media, we must be prepared to adapt to its ever-changing landscape. This dynamic environment evolves at a remarkably rapid pace, propelled by technological advancements and shifting user preferences. Hence, a keen foresight of emerging trends is an absolute necessity for public relations professionals in the making.

11.1. The Age of Artificial Intelligence and Automation

Artificial Intelligence (AI) and automation have lately garnered profound emphasis across industries. They are now aggressively penetrating the social media domain, yielding transformative impacts. AI integrated into social media platforms can assist in analyzing heaps of data, recognizing patterns, and predicting user behavior. This precise targeting can undoubtedly fuel deeply personalized communication strategies, a boon for public relations.

Chatbots, or virtual assistants, are notable ventures of AI in social media. These bots simulate human conversations and help businesses interact effectively with users, manage inquiries, and provide timely customer service, thereby bolstering public relations.

A captivating domain of AI, deep learning, holds immense potential for image and voice recognition. It could enable content analysis in posts or comments to assess sentiment, fortifying reputation management.

Moving on to automation, it can streamline various tasks such as scheduled posting or reporting, thus stepping up efficiency. Such advancements could revolutionize the dynamics of public relations on social media.

11.2. Rise of Augmented and Virtual Reality

In recent years, Augmented Reality (AR) and Virtual Reality (VR) have emerged as influential tools in the social media landscape. They enhance user experience with immersive content, allowing businesses a unique opportunity to engage their audience in novel, interactive ways.

VR facilitation in social media can provide users an immersive virtual environment to interact with the product or service, creating a more profound impression. AR, on the other hand, introduces virtual elements to the user's real world, adding a stimulating layer to their interaction.

Such immersive experiences could work wonders to amplify brand messaging and foster more meaningful connections with the audience. As a result, these technologies are crucial for future-facing public relations strategies.

11.3. Evolution of Content: Video and Live Streaming

The current wave of digital consumption suggests a massive upswing in video content. As the saying goes, a picture is worth a thousand words, and by inference, a video is priceless.

Live streaming is another trend gathering momentum. Real-time videos have the power to create more intimate engagement, driving genuine human connections. Brands can leverage live videos for virtual events, product launches, behind-the-scenes sneak peeks, or Q&A sessions, paving the way for interactive and transparent public relations.

11.4. The Growing Emphasis on Privacy and Security

Amidst the digital revolution, users are becoming increasingly aware of their privacy and the security of their data. They prioritize platforms that guarantee secure interactions and safeguard their sensitive information. In the spotlight also are privacy-related regulatory changes, demanding social platforms to bolster their data management protocols.

Public relations professionals must bear in mind these data ethics and the importance of maintaining reliability with their audience. It is critical to respect user privacy and ensure compliance with ever-tightening data protection policies.

11.5. The Thrust on Empathy and Authenticity

In the evolving social media architecture, empathy and authenticity are emerging as important pillars. Brands are expected to demonstrate genuine understanding and respect for their audiences' values, opinions, and challenges. Going beyond promotional messages, there is an increasing demand for brands to address social and environmental issues, and exhibit authenticity in their actions.

A public relations strategy deeply engaging with its audience, driven by empathy and authenticity, can fortify a brand's reputation, earn trust, and foster loyal followership in the long run.

In conclusion, these trends underline the vibrant and evolving vista of social media. In this fast-paced ecology, the ability to spot trends and adapt swiftly could be the game-changer for an effective public relations strategy. This instils the requirement for continuous learning, unwavering vigilance, nimble prudence, and strategic creativity to future-proof your organization's public relations endeavors in this interconnected digital world.

This chapter's blueprint should serve as a reliable compass, guiding you through the dynamic terrains of social media. Remember, the future is now. Arm yourself with these insights to power a deeply mindful, comprehensive and future-ready social media strategy for your public relations narrative.